Reader's Theater

Classic Poetry

2nd Edition

Susan Brown

Warm Hearts Publishing

Special thanks to Mary Rose. Your creativity, enthusiasm, and theatrical ideas are an inspiration to me.

Reader's Theater: Classic Poetry by Susan Brown

Copyright © 2014 by Susan Brown. All rights reserved.

Warm Hearts Publishing

Terms of Use:
The purchase of this material entitles the buyer to reproduce the pages for homeschool, classroom and small group use only. The reproduction of this book for an entire school or district is prohibited. Reproduction of these pages for other larger groups of more than 50 people requires the prior written consent of the author.

ISBN 978-1-939869-08-1

Disclaimer:
Any perceived slights of specific persons, peoples, or organizations in this book are unintentional.

2nd Edition

Portions of this book are based on text from the following works:

One Thousand Poems for Children: A Choice of the Best Verse Old and New. Edited by Roger Ingpen.
Child Songs of Cheer. Written by Evaleen Stein.
Symphonies and Their Meaning: Third Series: Modern Symphonies. Written by Philip Henry Goepp.
A Nonsense Anthology. Collected by Carolyn Wells.
Nonsense Songs: Stories, Botany and Alphabets. Written by Edward Lear.
Laughable Lyrics. Written by Edward Lear.
Little Men: Life at Plumfield with Joe's Boys. Written by Louisa May Alcott.

For information on how to purchase more copies of this book or to learn about our other products, please visit: www.WarmHeartsPublishing.com

Introduction

What is Reader's Theater?

Reader's Theater is the oral presentation of a written work that is performed with two or more readers. Memorization is not required because the focus of this form of drama is on *reading* the work with expression rather than reciting it. The readers help the audience to understand and visualize the text through their vocal performance.

Benefits of Using Reader's Theater

- It gives purpose to reading.
- It helps children develop reading fluency through repetition.
- It increases comprehension since the text must be interpreted for performance.
- It motivates children to read.
- It improves not only reading skills, but listening and speaking skills as well.
- It encourages children to work together.
- Performing Reader's Theater helps increase self-confidence.

Tips for Teaching Children How to Perform Reader's Theater

- Encourage the children to read with expression and to enunciate the words clearly.
- Teach the children how to project their voices so that they can be heard. Good posture helps with this.
- Pacing is important. Remind the children that they must be careful not to read too fast nor too slow, especially on unison parts.
- Show children how the script should be held. It's best if it is positioned below chin level so that the audience can see the faces of the performers. You may want to put the scripts in a three ring binder or attach them to construction paper or card stock for ease of use.
- Explain the importance of using facial expressions and gestures. This will make the presentation more interesting for the audience.
- Costumes and props may be used if desired, but are not a requirement.
- The positions of each reader on stage is up to you and the performers. Keep in mind that the scripts were written with the concept of having Reader 1 on the audience's left and the rest of the readers standing in number order to the right.
- Practice makes perfect, especially on unison parts. Encourage the children to rehearse their parts both individually and with their group.

What You'll Find in This Book

This book contains scripts for 2 - 8 readers. The pieces are grouped into sections according to the number of readers required for each performance. Some works have been modified to make them more suitable for Reader's Theater. "The Akond of Swat," for example has been abridged and broken up into two pieces due to its length. While these scripts were created with Reader's Theater in mind, they could also potentially be memorized and used for other forms of dramatic presentation.

Where to Find More Scripts

If you like these scripts, you can find more on our website at www.WarmHeartsPublishing.com.

Also, if you would like to share your success stories with me, offer suggestions, or ask questions, please visit the Contact page on the Warm Hearts Publishing website. I would love to hear from you.

Contents

Scripts for Two Readers 1
    Who Has Seen the Wind? 3
    Playgrounds 4
    The Shadows 5
    The Teapot Dragon 6
    The Picture-Book Giant 7
    What if? 8
    Our Tree Toad 9
    In July 10
    Zip! 11
    The Pelican Chorus 12

Scripts for Three Readers 15
    White Butterflies 17
    I Write About the Butterfly 18
    The City Mouse and the Garden Mouse 19
    The Canary 20
    Oxfordshire Children's May Song 21
    The Snail 22
    The Kitten at Play 24
    Our Puppies 25
    Did You Ever? 26
    Fairies 27
    Popcorn 28
    The Bird's Bath 29
    The Red Bird 30

Scripts for Four Readers 31
    Foolish Flowers 33
    The Chorus of Frogs 34
    The Reformation of Godfrey Gore 36
    How the Little Kite Learned to Fly 38
    Mr. Nobody 40
    You Spotted Snakes 42
    The Fountain 43
    An Apple Orchard in the Spring 45
    Winter Night 47
    In the Water-World 48
    Calico Pie 50
    The Akond of Swat - Part 1 52
    The Akond of Swat - Part 2 55

Scripts for Five or More Readers 59
    Deeds of Kindness 61
    Try Again 63
    The Dream of a Girl Who Lived at Seven-Oaks 65
    Going Downhill on a Bicycle 66
    Twenty Froggies 67

P's and Q's	68
The Boy and the Wolf	69
The Lion and the Mouse	71
The Grass	73
The Jovial Welshmen	74
The Sorcerer's Apprentice	77

Scripts for Two Readers

Who Has Seen the Wind?

Christina Georgina Rossetti

.... **CHARACTERS** ....

READER 1 READER 2

....

READER 1: Who has seen the wind?

UNISON: Neither I nor you:

READER 1: But when the leaves hang trembling,
　　　　　　The wind is passing through.

READER 2: Who has seen the wind?

UNISON: Neither you nor I:

READER 2: But when the trees bow down their heads,
　　　　　　The wind is passing by.

Playgrounds

Laurence Alma-Tadema

CHARACTERS

READER 1 READER 2

READER 1: In summer I am very glad
    We children are so small,

READER 2: For we can see a thousand things
    That men can't see at all.

READER 1: They don't know much about the moss
    And all the stones they pass:

READER 2: They never lie and play among
    The forests in the grass:

READER 1: They walk about a long way off;
    And, when we're at the sea,

READER 2: Let father stoop as best he can
    He can't find things like me.

READER 1: But, when the snow is on the ground
    And all the puddles freeze,

READER 2: I wish that I were very tall,
    High up above the trees.

The Shadows

Mary Lundie Duncan

.... **CHARACTERS** ....

MAMMA   CHILD

....

MAMMA: The candles are lighted, the fire blazes bright,
    The curtains are drawn to keep out the cold air;
What makes you so grave, little darling, tonight,
    And where is your smile, little quiet one, where?

CHILD: Mamma, I see something so dark on the wall,
    It moves up and down, and it looks very strange;
Sometimes it is large, and sometimes it is small;
    Pray tell me, what is it, and why does it change?

MAMMA: It is mamma's shadow that puzzles you so,
    And there is your own close beside it, my love;
Now run round the room, it will go where you go;
    When you sit, 'twill be still, when you rise, it will move.

CHILD: I don't like to see it, do please let me ring
    For Betsy to take all the shadows away.

MAMMA: No; Betsy oft carries a heavier thing,
    But she could not lift this, should she try a whole day.

These wonderful shadows are caused by the light
    From fire and from candles upon us that falls;
Were we not sitting here, all that place would be bright,
    But the light can't shine through us, you know, on the walls.

And, when you are out some fine day in the sun,
    I'll take you where shadows of apple trees lie;
And houses and cottages too, every one
    Casts a shade when the sun's shining bright in the sky.

CHILD: O yes! I thank you for telling me this plain;
    I'll not be afraid of a shadow again.

The Teapot Dragon
Rupert Sargent Holland

······································ **CHARACTERS** ······································

                READER 1   READER 2

··

READER 1:   There's a dragon on our teapot,
                  With a long and crinkly tail,
            His claws are like a pincer bug,
                  His wings are like a sail;

READER 2:   His tongue is always sticking out,
                  And so I used to think
            He must be very hungry, or
                  He wanted tea to drink.

READER 1:   But once when Mother wasn't round
                  I dipped my fingers in,
            And when I pulled them out I found
                  I'd blistered all the skin.

READER 2:   Now when I see the dragon crawl
                  Around our china pot,
            I know he's burned his tongue because
                  The water is

UNISON: so hot.

The Picture-Book Giant
Evaleen Stein

CHARACTERS
NARRATOR   GIANT

NARRATOR: Once there was a fierce, defiant,
Greedy, grumpy, grizzly giant
In the pages of a picture-book, and he
Sometimes screamed, in sudden rages,

GIANT: "I must jump out from these pages,
For this life's a much too humdrum one for me!
Fiddle-dee!
Yes, this life's a bit too quiet one for me!"

NARRATOR: So one rainy day he did it,
Took the picture-book and hid it,
Stamped his foot, and shouting loudly,

GIANT: "Now I'm free!"

NARRATOR: Boldly started out, forgetting
That he could not stand a wetting!
He was just a paper giant, don't you see?
Dearie me!
Just a gaudy, picture giant, don't you see?

What if?

Evaleen Stein

CHARACTERS

READER 1   READER 2

READER 1: When I see the new moon lightly
　　　　　　Through cloud ripples slip,

READER 2: Then I'm sure that shining brightly
　　　　　　It's a fairy ship!

READER 1: What if in it we were sailing
　　　　　　Far and far away,

READER 2: With a wake of silver trailing,
　　　　　　Till the golden day?

READER 1: Why, we'd fly back home together
　　　　　　Safely from the sky,

READER 2: For the moon's a fairy feather
　　　　　　When the sun is high!

Our Tree Toad
Evaleen Stein

.... **CHARACTERS** ....

NARRATOR GRANDFATHER

....

NARRATOR: Grandfather says the tree toad,
　　That to our yard has come,
Is just a little wee toad
　　No bigger than his thumb!

And that his coat's so queer it
　　Can turn from green to blue!
Whatever color's near it,
　　Why, that's its color, too!

And then Grandfather snickers
　　And says,

GRANDFATHER: "Would you suppose
He climbs with little stickers
　　On all his little toes?

And don't you wish your toes now
　　Were fixed like his? For, see,
Right up the elm he goes now
　　And sticks tight to the tree!

But then,"

NARRATOR: he says,

GRANDFATHER: "O dear me!
　　If all the little boys
Could screech as loud, I fear me
　　There'd be a dreadful noise!"

In July

Evaleen Stein

CHARACTERS

READER 1　　　　　READER 2

READER 1:　Let us find a shady wady
　　　　　　　Pretty little brook;

READER 2:　Let us have some candy handy,
　　　　　　　And a picture book.

READER 1:　There all day we'll stay and play and
　　　　　　　Never mind the heat,

READER 2:　While the water gleaming, streaming,
　　　　　　　Ripples round our feet.

READER 1:　And we'll gather curly pearly
　　　　　　　Mussel shells while bright

READER 2:　Frightened minnows darting, parting,
　　　　　　　Scurry out of sight.

READER 1:　What if, what if,

UNISON:　heigh ho! my oh!

READER 2:　All the "ifs" were true,

READER 1:　And the little fishes wishes,

READER 2:　Now, what would you do?

Zip!

Evaleen Stein

························ **CHARACTERS** ························

READER 1 READER 2

··

READER 1: When we went to drive the cows home
                Down the lane today,

READER 2: There was such a funny bunny
                Jumped across the way!

READER 1: All we saw as he ran past us,
                Faster than a quail,

READER 2: Was his snow white fuzzy-wuzzy
                Little

UNISON: cotton tail!

The Pelican Chorus

Edward Lear

.... **CHARACTERS** ....

READER 1   READER 2

....

READER 1: King and Queen of the Pelicans we;
           No other Birds so grand we see!

READER 2: None but we have feet like fins!
           With lovely leathery throats and chins!

UNISON: Ploffskin, Pluffskin, Pelican jee!

READER 1: We think no Birds so happy as we!

UNISON: Plumpskin, Ploshkin, Pelican Jill!

READER 2: We think so then, and we thought so still!

READER 1: We live on the Nile. The Nile we love.
           By night we sleep on the cliffs above;

READER 2: By day we fish, and at eve we stand
           On long bare islands of yellow sand.

READER 1: And when the sun sinks slowly down,
           And the great rock walls grow dark and brown,

READER 2: Where the purple river rolls fast and dim
           And the Ivory Ibis starlike skim,

READER 1: Wing to wing we dance around,
           Stamping our feet with a flumpy sound,

READER 2: Opening our mouths as Pelicans ought;
           And this is the song we nightly snort,

UNISON: Ploffskin, Pluffskin, Pelican jee!

READER 1: We think no Birds so happy as we!

UNISON: Plumpskin, Ploshkin, Pelican Jill!

READER 2: We think so then, and we thought so still!

Scripts for Three Readers

White Butterflies

Algernon Charles Swinburne

.... **CHARACTERS** ....

READER 1 READER 3
READER 2

....

READER 1: Fly, white butterflies, out to sea,

READER 2: Frail pale wings for the winds to try,

READER 3: Small white wings that we scarce can see,

UNISON: Fly!

READER 3: Some fly light as a laugh of glee,

READER 2: Some fly soft as a long, low sigh;

READER 1: All to the haven where each would be,

UNISON: Fly!

I Write About the Butterfly

Louisa May Alcott

.... **CHARACTERS** ....

READER 1   READER 3
READER 2

....

READER 1: I write about the butterfly,
        It is a pretty thing;
    And flies about like the birds,
        But it does not sing.

READER 2: First it is a little grub,
        And then it is a nice yellow cocoon,
    And then the butterfly
        Eats its way out soon.

READER 3: They live on dew and honey,
        They do not have any hive,
    They do not sting like wasps,

READER 2: and bees,

READER 1: and hornets,

READER 3: And to be as good as they are

  UNISON: we should strive.

The City Mouse and the Garden Mouse

Christina Georgina Rossetti

························· **CHARACTERS** ·························

      READER 1   READER 3

      READER 2

··

READER 1: The city mouse lives in a house;

READER 3: The garden mouse lives in a bower,

READER 2: He's friendly with the frogs and toads,
                  And sees the pretty plants in flower.

READER 1: The city mouse eats bread and cheese;

READER 3: The garden mouse eats what he can;

READER 2: We will not grudge him seeds and stalks,
                  Poor little timid furry man.

The Canary
Elizabeth Turner

CHARACTERS

READER 1   READER 3
READER 2

READER 1: Mary had a little bird,
                With feathers bright and yellow,

READER 2: Slender legs, upon my word,
                He was a pretty fellow!

READER 3: Sweetest notes he always sung,
                Which much delighted Mary;

READER 2: Often where his cage was hung,
                She sat to hear Canary.

READER 3: Crumbs of bread and dainty seeds
                She carried to him daily;

READER 1: Seeking for the early weeds,
                She decked his palace gaily.

READER 3: This, my little readers, learn,

READER 2: And ever practice duly;

READER 1: Songs and smiles of love return

UNISON: To friends who love you truly.

Oxfordshire Children's May Song

This is a country rhyme

CHARACTERS

READER 1 READER 3
READER 2

UNISON: Spring is coming, spring is coming,

READER 1: Birdies, build your nest;
Weave together straw and feather,
Doing each your best.

UNISON: Spring is coming, spring is coming,

READER 2: Flowers are coming too:

READER 1: Pansies,

READER 2: lilies,

READER 3: daffodillies,

READER 2: Now are coming through.

UNISON: Spring is coming, spring is coming,

READER 3: All around is fair;
Shimmer and quiver on the river,
Joy is everywhere.

UNISON: We wish you a happy May.

The Snail

From the Latin of Vincent Bourne, translated by William Cowper

·· **CHARACTERS** ··

          READER 1   READER 3

          READER 2

READER 1: To grass or leaf, or fruit or wall,
The snail sticks close, nor fears to fall,
As if he grew there, house and all

UNISON: Together.

READER 2: Within that house secure he hides,
When danger imminent betides,
Of storm, or other harm besides

UNISON: Of weather.

READER 3: Give but his horns the slightest touch,
His self-collecting power is such,
He shrinks into his house with much

UNISON: Displeasure.

READER 1: Wherever he dwells, he dwells alone,
Except himself has chattels none,
Well satisfied to be his own

UNISON: Whole treasure.

READER 2: Thus hermit-like, his life he leads,
Nor partner of his banquet needs,
And if he meets one only feeds

UNISON: The faster.

READER 3: Who seeks him must be worse than blind,
(He and his house are so combined),
If, finding it, he fails to find

UNISON: Its master.

The Kitten at Play

William Wordsworth

························· **CHARACTERS** ·························

          READER 1   READER 3
          READER 2

··

READER 1: See the kitten on the wall,
               Sporting with the leaves that fall,

READER 2: Withered leaves, one, two and three,
               Falling from the elder-tree,

READER 3: Through the calm and frosty air
               Of the morning bright and fair.

READER 2: See the kitten, how she starts,

READER 1: Crouches,

READER 3: stretches,

READER 2: paws and darts;

READER 3: With a tiger-leap half way
               Now she meets her coming prey.

READER 1: Lets it go as fast, and then
               Has it in her power again.

READER 3: Now she works with three and four,
               Like a little conjurer;

READER 2: Quick as he in feats of art,
               Gracefully she plays her part;

READER 1: Yet were gazing thousands there,

UNISON: What would little Tabby care?

Our Puppies

Evaleen Stein

CHARACTERS

READER 1
READER 2
READER 3

READER 1: Little ears as soft as silk,

READER 3: Little teeth as white as milk,

READER 2: Little noses cool and pink,

READER 3: Little eyes that blink and blink,

READER 1: Little bodies round and fat,

READER 2: Little hearts that pit-a-pat,

UNISON: Surely prettier puppies never
Were before nor can be ever!

Did You Ever?

Evaleen Stein

··· **CHARACTERS** ···

        READER 1   READER 3

        READER 2

···

READER 1: Did you ever see a fairy in a rose leaf coat and cap
Swinging in a cobweb hammock as he napped his noonday nap?

READER 2: Did you ever see one waken very thirsty and drink up
All the honey dew that glimmered in a golden buttercup?

READER 3: Did you ever see one fly away on rainbow twinkling wings?
If you did not,

UNISON: why,

READER 3: how comes it that you never see such things?

Fairies

Evaleen Stein

CHARACTERS

READER 1   READER 3
READER 2

READER 1: Grandfather says that sometimes,
    When stars are twinkling and
A new moon shines, there come times
    When folks see fairyland!

READER 2: So when there's next a new moon,
    I mean to watch all night!
Grandfather says a blue moon
    Is best for fairy light,

READER 3: And in a peach bloom, maybe,
    If I look I shall see
A little fairy baby
    No bigger than a bee!

Popcorn

Evaleen Stein

CHARACTERS

READER 1   READER 3
READER 2

READER 1: Pop!

READER 2: Pop!

READER 3: Poppetty-pop!

READER 1: Shake and rattle and rattle and shake
The golden grains as they bounce and break

READER 3: To fluffy puffiness. Poppetty-pop!
Bursting and banging the popper's top!

UNISON: Poppetty-pop! Pop! Pop!

READER 2: The yellow kernels, oh, see them grow
White as cotton or flakes of snow!

UNISON: Pop! Pop!

READER 3: O ho, how they frolic and fly about
And turn themselves suddenly inside out!

UNISON: Pop-pop-poppetty! Pop-pop-pop!

READER 1: The popper's full and we'll have to stop;

READER 2: Pile the bowl with the tempting treat,

UNISON: Children, come, it is time to eat!

The Bird's Bath

Evaleen Stein

·· **CHARACTERS** ··

          READER 1   READER 3

          READER 2

···

READER 1: In our garden we have made
                Such a pretty little pool,

READER 2: Lined with pebbles neatly laid,
                Filled with water clean and cool.

READER 3: When the sun shines warm and high
                Robins cluster round its brink,

READER 2: Never one comes flying by
                But will flutter down to drink.

READER 3: Then they splash

READER 1: and splash

READER 2: and splash,

READER 1: Spattering little showers bright

READER 3: All around, till off they flash
                Singing sweetly their delight.

The Red Bird
Evaleen Stein

.... **CHARACTERS** ....

        READER 1   READER 3

        READER 2

....

READER 1: Swept lightly by the south wind
                The elm leaves softly stirred,

READER 3: And in their pale green clusters
                There straightway bloomed a bird!

READER 2: His glossy feathers glistened
                With dyes as richly red

READER 3: As any tulip flaming
                From out the garden bed.

READER 1: But ah, unlike the tulips,
                In joyous strain, ere long,

READER 2: This red bird flower unfolded
                A heart of golden song!

Scripts for Four Readers

Foolish Flowers

Rupert Sargent Holland

CHARACTERS

READER 1　　　　READER 3
READER 2　　　　READER 4

READER 1:　We've Foxgloves in our garden;
　　　　　　　　How careless they must be
　　　　　　To leave their gloves out hanging

UNISON:　Where everyone can see!

READER 2:　And Bachelors leave their Buttons
　　　　　　　　In the same careless way,
　　　　　　If I should do the same with mine,

UNISON:　What would mother say?

READER 3:　We've lots of Larkspurs in the yard,
　　　　　　　　Larks only fly and sing,
　　　　　　Birds surely don't need spurs because

UNISON:　They don't ride anything!

READER 4:　And as for Johnny-Jump-Ups,
　　　　　　　　I saw a hornet light
　　　　　　On one of them the other day,

UNISON:　He didn't jump a mite!

The Chorus of Frogs

Anne Hawkshaw

.... **CHARACTERS** ....

     FROG 1   FROG 3
     FROG 2   NARRATOR

....

FROG 1: "Ribbit, ribbit, ribbit!"

NARRATOR: Said the croaking voice of a frog:

FROG 1: "A rainy day
  In the month of May,
   And plenty of room in the bog."

FROG 2: "Ribbit, ribbit, ribbit!"

NARRATOR: Said the frog, as it hopped away:

FROG 2: "The insects feed
  On the floating weed,
   And I'm hungry for dinner today."

FROG 3: "Ribbit, ribbit, ribbit!"

NARRATOR: Said the frog, as it splashed about:

FROG 3: "Good neighbours all,
  When you hear me call,
   It is odd that you don't come out."

ALL FROGS: "Ribbit, ribbit, ribbit!"

NARRATOR: Said the frogs:

FROG 1: "it is charming weather;

FROG 2: We'll come and sup

FROG 3:   When the moon is up,

ALL FROGS: And we'll all of us croak together."

The Reformation of Godfrey Gore

William Brighty Rands

··· **CHARACTERS** ···

| PARENT 1 | GODFREY |
| PARENT 2 | NARRATOR |

··

NARRATOR: Godfrey Gordon Gustavus Gore.
No doubt you have heard the name before,
Was a boy who never would shut a door!

The wind might whistle, the wind might roar,
And teeth be aching and throats be sore,
But still he never would shut the door.

His father would beg, his mother implore,

PARENTS: "Godfrey Gordon Gustavus Gore,
(2 readers) We really do wish you would shut the door!"

NARRATOR: Their hands they wrung, their hair they tore;
But Godfrey Gordon Gustavus Gore
Was deaf as the buoy out at the Nore.

When he walked forth the folks would roar,

PARENTS: "Godfrey Gordon Gustavus Gore,
Why don't you think to shut the door?"

NARRATOR: They rigged up a Shutter with sail and oar,
And threatened to pack off Gustavus Gore
On a voyage of penance to Singapore.

But he begged for mercy and said,

GODFREY: "No more!
Pray do not send me to Singapore
On a Shutter, and then I will shut the door!"

PARENTS: "You will?"

NARRATOR: said his parents;

PARENTS: "then keep on shore!
But mind you do! For the plague is sore
Of a fellow that never will shut the door,
Godfrey Gordon Gustavus Gore!"

How the Little Kite Learned to Fly

Author unknown

.... **CHARACTERS** ....

        NARRATOR 1   LITTLE KITE
        NARRATOR 2   BIG KITE

....

LITTLE KITE: "I never can do it,"

NARRATOR 1: the little kite said,
As he looked at the others high over his head;

LITTLE KITE: "I know I should fall if I tried to fly."

BIG KITE: "Try,"

NARRATOR 2: said the big kite;

BIG KITE: "only try,
Or I fear you never will learn at all."

NARRATOR 1: But the little kite said,

LITTLE KITE: "I'm afraid I'll fall."

NARRATOR 2: The big kite nodded:

BIG KITE: "Ah, well, good-bye.
I'm off."

NARRATOR 1: and he rose toward the tranquil sky.

NARRATOR 2: Then the little kite's paper stirred at the sight,
And trembling he shook himself free for flight.

NARRATOR 1: First whirling and frightened, then braver grown,
Up, up, he rose through the air alone,

NARRATOR 2: Till the big kite looking down could see
The little one rising steadily.

NARRATOR 1: Then how the little kite thrilled with pride,
As he sailed with the big kite side by side!

NARRATOR 2: While far below, he could see the ground,
And the boys like small spots moving round.

NARRATOR 1: They rested high in the quiet air,
And only the birds and clouds were there.

LITTLE KITE: "Oh, how happy I am!"

NARRATOR 2: the little kite cried;

LITTLE KITE: "And all because I was brave, and tried."

Mr. Nobody

Author unknown

CHARACTERS

READER 1   READER 3
READER 2   READER 4

READER 1: I know a funny little man,
               As quiet as a mouse,

READER 3: Who does the mischief that is done
               In everybody's house!

READER 2: There's no one ever sees his face,
               And yet we all agree

READER 4: That every plate we break was cracked

UNISON: By Mr. Nobody.

READER 3: 'Tis he who always tears out books,
               Who leaves the door ajar,

READER 2: He pulls the buttons from our shirts,
               And scatters pins afar;

READER 4: That squeaking door will always squeak,
               For prithee, don't you see,

READER 1: We leave the oiling to be done

UNISON: By Mr. Nobody.

READER 2: He puts damp wood upon the fire,
               That kettles cannot boil;

READER 4: His are the feet that bring in mud,
               And all the carpets soil.

READER 3:   The papers always are mislaid,
                   Who had them last but he?

READER 1:   There's no one tosses them about

UNISON: But Mr. Nobody.

READER 4:   The finger marks upon the door
                   By none of us are made;

READER 2:   We never leave the blinds unclosed,
                   To let the curtains fade.

READER 1:   The ink we never spill, the boots
                   That lying round you see

READER 3:   Are not our boots; they all belong

UNISON: To Mr. Nobody.

You Spotted Snakes

From *A Midsummer Night's Dream*, Act II. Scene 2, by William Shakespeare

.... **CHARACTERS** ....

        FAIRY 1   CHORUS MEMBERS

        FAIRY 2

....

FAIRY 1: You spotted snakes, with double tongue,
                Thorny hedgehogs, be not seen;
           Newts and blind-worms, do no wrong;
                Come not near our fairy queen.

CHORUS: Philomel, with melody
(2 or more Sing in our sweet lullaby;
children) Lulla, lulla, lullaby; lulla, lulla, lullaby:
            Never harm,
           Nor spell nor charm,
           Come our lovely lady nigh;
           So, good night, with lullaby.

FAIRY 2: Weaving spiders, come not here;
                Hence, you long-legged spinners, hence!
           Beetles black, approach not near;
                Worm, nor snail, do no offence.

CHORUS: Philomel, with melody
           Sing in our sweet lullaby;
           Lulla, lulla, lullaby; lulla, lulla, lullaby:
           Never harm,
           Nor spell nor charm,
           Come our lovely lady nigh;
           So, good night, with lullaby.

The Fountain

James Russell Lowell

CHARACTERS

READER 1 READER 3
READER 2 READER 4

READER 1: Into the sunshine,

READER 3: Full of the light,

READER 2: Leaping and flashing

READER 4: From morn till night!

READER 3: Into the moonlight,

READER 2: Whiter than snow,

READER 4: Waving so flower-like

READER 1: When the winds blow!

READER 2: Into the starlight,

READER 4: Rushing in spray,

READER 3: Happy at midnight,

READER 1: Happy by day!

READER 4: Ever in motion,

READER 2: Blithesome and cheery,

READER 1: Still climbing heavenward,

READER 3: Never aweary;

READER 2: Glad of all weathers,

READER 1: Still seeming best,

READER 4: Upward or downward

READER 3: Motion thy rest;

READER 1: Full of a nature

READER 4: Nothing can tame,

READER 2: Changed every moment,

READER 3: Ever the same;

READER 4: Ceaseless aspiring,

READER 3: Ceaseless content,

READER 1: Darkness or sunshine

READER 2: Thy element;

UNISON: Glorious fountain!

READER 1: Let my heart be

READER 2: Fresh,

READER 3: changeful,

READER 4: constant,

UNISON: Upward, like thee!

An Apple Orchard in the Spring

William Martin

CHARACTERS

READER 1 READER 3
READER 2 READER 4

READER 1: Have you seen an apple orchard in the spring?

READERS 2, 3, 4: In the spring?

READER 1: An English apple orchard in the spring?
    When the spreading trees are flowery
    With their wealth of promised glory,
    And the mavis sings its story,

READERS 2, 3, 4: In the spring.

READER 2: Have you plucked the apple blossoms in the spring?

READERS 1, 3, 4: In the spring?

READER 2: And caught their subtle odors in the spring?
    Pink buds pouting at the light,
    Crumpled petals baby-white,
    Just to touch them a delight,

READERS 1, 3, 4: In the spring.

READER 3: Have you walked beneath the blossoms in the spring?

READERS 1, 2, 4: In the spring?

READER 3: Beneath the apple blossoms in the spring?
    When the pink cascades are falling,
    And the silver brooklets brawling,
    And the cuckoo bird soft calling,

READERS 1, 2, 4: In the spring.

READER 4:   If you have not, then you know not, in the spring,

READERS 1, 2, 3:   In the spring,

READER 4:   Half the color, beauty, wonder of the spring,
　　　　　　　No sweet sight can I remember
　　　　　　　Half so precious, half so tender,
　　　　　　　As the apple blossoms render

READERS 1, 2, 3:   In the spring.

Winter Night

Mary F. Butts

.... **CHARACTERS** ....

READER 1 READER 3
READER 2 READER 4

UNISON: Blow, wind, blow!

READER 1: Drift the flying snow!
    Send it twirling, whirling overhead!
      There's a bedroom in a tree
      Where, snug as snug can be,
    The squirrel nests in his cosy bed.

UNISON: Shriek, wind, shriek!

READER 2: Make the branches creak!
    Battle with the boughs till break o' day!
      In a snow-cave warm and tight,
      Through the icy winter night
    The rabbit sleeps the peaceful hours away.

UNISON: Call, wind, call,

READER 3: In entry and in hall,
    Straight from off the mountain white and wild!
      Soft purrs the pussy-cat
      On her little fluffy mat,
    And beside her nestles close her furry child.

UNISON: Scold, wind, scold,

READER 4: So bitter and so bold!
    Shake the windows with your tap, tap, tap!
      With half-shut, dreamy eyes
      The drowsy baby lies
    Cuddled closely in his mother's lap.

In the Water World

Evaleen Stein

························· **CHARACTERS** ·························

           READER 1   READER 3

           READER 2   READER 4

··

READER 1: Down among the water weeds,
              Darting through the grass,

READER 2: Round about the tasseled reeds,
              See the minnows pass!

READER 3: See the little turtles there,
              Hiding, half asleep,

READER 4: Tucked in tangled mosses where
              Tiny crayfish

UNISON: creep!

READER 2: Watch the trailing grasses string
              Strands of purple shells

READER 3: That the lazy ripples ring,
              Sweet as silver bells;

READER 1: Watch the sunshine sift and drift
              Down the eddy whirls,

READER 4: Whence the laden white weeds lift
              Loads of blossom pearls;

READER 3: While the limpid shadows slip

UNISON: Softly
(whispered)

READER 3: in between,

READER 1: And the pussy willows dip
               Lightly in the green

READER 4: Of the mocking trees that grow
               Down the water sky,

READER 2: Flecked with fleecy clouds that blow
               Where the reed birds fly.

READER 4: Oh, such marvels manifold
               Fill the summer stream,

READER 3: Such enticing things untold
               Through the ripples gleam,

READER 2: If you could a moment turn
               Into what you wish,

READER 1: Would it not be

UNISON: fun

READER 1: to be
               Yonder little fish?

Calico Pie

Edward Lear

·· **CHARACTERS** ··

        READER 1   READER 3

        READER 2   READER 4

··

READER 1: Calico pie,
The little birds fly

READER 2: Down to the calico-tree:

READER 3: Their wings were blue,
And they sang "Tilly-loo!"
Till away they flew;

READER 4: And they never came back to me!

UNISON: They never came back,
They never came back,
They never came back to me!

READER 2: Calico jam,
The little Fish swam

READER 4: Over the Syllabub Sea.

READER 1: He took off his hat
To the Sole and the Sprat,
And the Willeby-wat:

READER 3: But he never came back to me;

UNISON: He never came back,
He never came back,
He never came back to me.

READER 3: Calico ban,
The little Mice ran

READER 1: To be ready in time for tea;

READER 4: Flippity flup,
They drank it all up,
And danced in the cup:

READER 2: But they never came back to me;

UNISON: They never came back,
They never came back,
They never came back to me.

READER 4: Calico drum,
The Grasshoppers come,

READER 3: The Butterfly, Beetle, and Bee,

READER 2: Over the ground,
Around and round,
With a hop and a bound;

READER 1: But they never came back,

UNISON: They never came back,
They never came back.
They never came back to me.

The Akond of Swat - Part 1
Edward Lear

CHARACTERS

READER 1 READER 3
READER 2 READER 4

READER 1: Who,

READER 2: or why,

READER 3: or which,

READER 4: or what,

UNISON: Is the Akond of Swat?

READER 2: Is he tall or short,

READER 4: or dark or fair?

READER 3: Does he sit on a stool or sofa or chair,

READER 1: or Squat,

UNISON: The Akond of Swat?

READER 4: Is he wise or foolish,

READER 2: young or old?

READER 1: Does he drink his soup and his coffee cold,

READER 3: or Hot,

UNISON: The Akond of Swat?

READER 1: Does he sing or whistle,

READER 4: jabber or talk,

READER 2: And when riding abroad does he gallop or walk,

READER 3: or Trot,

UNISON: The Akond of Swat?

READER 4: Does he wear a turban,

READER 3: a fez

READER 1: or a hat?

READER 2: Does he sleep on a mattress,

READER 4: a bed

READER 3: or a mat,

READER 1: or a Cot,

UNISON: The Akond of Swat?

READER 3: When he writes a copy in round hand size,

READER 1: Does he cross his t's

READER 4: and finish his i's

READER 2: with a Dot,

UNISON: The Akond of Swat?

READER 1: Can he write a letter concisely clear,

READER 3: Without a speck

READER 2: or a smudge

READER 4: or smear

READER 1: or Blot,

UNISON: The Akond of Swat?

READER 4: Do his people like him extremely well?

READER 1: Or do they,

READER 2: whenever they can,

READER 3: rebel,

READER 4: or Plot,

UNISON: At the Akond of Swat?

READER 2: Does he study the wants of his own dominion?

READER 3: Or doesn't he care for public opinion

READER 1: a Jot,

UNISON: The Akond of Swat?

READER 4: Some one, or nobody knows I wot

READER 1: Who

READER 2: or which

READER 3: or why

READER 4: or what

UNISON: Is the Akond of Swat!

The Akond of Swat - Part 2
Edward Lear

CHARACTERS

READER 1 READER 3
READER 2 READER 4

READER 1: Who,

READER 2: or why,

READER 3: or which,

READER 4: or what,

UNISON: Is the Akond of Swat?

READER 3: Does he wear a white tie

READER 1: when he dines with his friends,

READER 4: And tie it neat in a bow with ends,

READER 2: or a Knot,

UNISON: The Akond of Swat?

READER 1: Does he like new cream,

READER 3: and hate mince pies?

READER 2: When he looks at the sun does he wink his eyes,

READER 4: or Not,

UNISON: The Akond of Swat?

READER 3: To amuse his mind do his people show him

READER 2: Pictures,

READER 4: or any one's last new poem,

READER 1: or What,

UNISON: For the Akond of Swat?

READER 2: At night if he suddenly screams and wakes,

READER 1: Do they bring him only a few small cakes,

READER 3: or a Lot,

UNISON: For the Akond of Swat?

READER 4: Does he live on turnips,

READER 3: tea

READER 2: or tripe,

READER 1: Does he like his shawl to be marked with a stripe

READER 4: or a Dot,

UNISON: The Akond of Swat?

READER 2: Does he like to lie on his back in a boat

READER 3: Like the lady who lived in that isle remote,

READER 1: Shalott.

UNISON: The Akond of Swat?

READER 4: Does he like to sit by the calm blue wave?

READER 2: Or to sleep and snore in a dark green cave,

READER 3: or a Grott,

UNISON: The Akond of Swat?

READER 1: Does he teach his subjects to roast and bake?

READER 3: Does he sail about on an inland lake,

READER 2: in a Yacht,

UNISON: The Akond of Swat?

READER 4: Some one, or nobody knows I wot

READER 1: Who

READER 2: or which

READER 3: or why

READER 4: or what

UNISON: Is the Akond of Swat!

Scripts for Five or More Readers

Deeds of Kindness

Epes Sargent

······························· **CHARACTERS** ·······························

           READER 1   READER 4

           READER 2   READER 5

           READER 3   READER 6

··

READER 1: Suppose the little Cowslip
                Should hang its little cup
            And say,

READER 4: "I'm such a little flower
                I'd better not grow up!"

READER 2: How many a weary traveller
                Would miss it's fragrant smell?

READER 5: How many a little child would grieve
                To lose it from the dell!

READER 3: Suppose the glistening Dewdrop
                Upon the grass should say,

READER 6: "What can a little dewdrop do?
                I'd better roll away!"

READER 4: The blade on which it rested,
                Before the day was done,

READER 1: Without a drop to moisten it,
                Would wither in the sun.

READER 5: Suppose the little breezes,
                Upon a summer's day,

READER 2: Should think themselves too small to cool
                The traveller on his way.

READER 6:   Who would not miss the smallest,
                     And softest ones that blow,

READER 3:   And think they made a great mistake
                     If they were acting so?

READER 1:   How many deeds of kindness

READER 2:   A little child can do,

READER 3:   Although it has but little strength

READER 4:   And little wisdom too!

READER 5:   It wants a loving spirit

READER 6:   Much more than strength, to prove

UNISON: How many things a child can do
                  For others by its love.

Try Again
William Edward Hickson

.... **CHARACTERS** ....

          READER 1   READER 4
          READER 2   READER 5
          READER 3

....

READER 1: "Tis a lesson you should heed,

UNISON: Try again;

READER 3: If at first you don't succeed,

UNISON: Try again;

READER 5: Then your courage should appear,

READER 2: For if you will persevere,

READER 4: You will conquer, never fear,

UNISON: Try again.

READER 3: Once or twice, though you should fail,

UNISON: Try again;

READER 1: If you would at last prevail,

UNISON: Try again;

READER 5: If we strive, 'tis no disgrace

READER 4: Though we do not win the race;

READER 2: What should we do in that case?

UNISON: Try again.

READER 5: If you find your task is hard,

  UNISON: Try again;

READER 2: Time will bring you your reward,

  UNISON: Try again;

READER 3: All that other folk can do,

READER 1: Why, with patience, may not you?

READER 4: Only keep this rule in view,

  UNISON: Try again.

The Dream of a Girl Who Lived at Seven-Oaks

William Brighty Rands

CHARACTERS

READER 1	READER 4	READER 7
READER 2	READER 5	
READER 3	READER 6	

READER 1: Seven sweet singing birds up in a tree;

READER 4: Seven swift sailing ships white upon the sea;

READER 7: Seven slim racehorses ready for a run;

READER 3: Seven gold butterflies, flitting overhead;

READER 6: Seven red roses blowing in a garden bed;

READER 2: Seven white lilies, with honey bees inside them;

READER 5: Seven round rainbows with clouds to divide them;

UNISON: Seven nights running I dreamt it all plain;
With bread and jam for supper I could dream it all again!

Going Downhill on a Bicycle

Henry Charles Beeching

CHARACTERS

NARRATOR 1
NARRATOR 2
NARRATOR 3
NARRATOR 4
BOY

NARRATOR 1: With lifted feet, hands still,
I am poised, and down the hill

NARRATOR 2: Dart, with heedful mind;
The air goes by in a wind.

NARRATOR 3: Swifter and yet more swift,
Till the heart with a mighty lift

NARRATOR 4: Makes the lungs laugh, the throat cry:

BOY: "O bird, see; see, bird, I fly.
Is this, is this your joy?
O bird, then I, though a boy,
For a golden moment share
Your feathery life in air!"

NARRATOR 4: Say, heart, is there aught like this
In a world that is full of bliss?

NARRATOR 3: 'Tis more than skating, bound
Steel-shod to the level ground.

NARRATOR 2: Speed slackens now, I float
Awhile in my airy boat;

NARRATOR 1: Till, when the wheels scarce crawl,
My feet to the treadles fall.

Twenty Froggies

George Cooper

.... **CHARACTERS** ....

READER 1	READER 3	READER 5
READER 2	READER 4	

READER 1: Twenty froggies went to school
　　　　　　 Down beside a rushing pool.

READER 4: Twenty little coats of green,
　　　　　　 Twenty vests all white and clean.

UNISON:　 "We must be in time,"

READER 2: said they,

UNISON:　 "First we study, then we play;
　　　　　　 That is how we keep the rule,
　　　　　　 When we froggies go to school."

READER 3: Master Bullfrog, brave and stern,
　　　　　　 Called the classes in their turn,

READER 5: Taught them how to nobly strive,
　　　　　　 Also how to leap and dive;

READER 2: Taught them how to dodge a blow,
　　　　　　 From the stick that bad boys throw.

READER 4: Twenty froggies grew up fast,
　　　　　　 Bullfrogs they became at last;

READER 1: Polished in a high degree,
　　　　　　 As each froggie ought to be,

READER 5: Now they sit on other logs,

READER 3: Teaching other little frogs.

P's and Q's
Rupert Sargent Holland

.... **CHARACTERS** ....

READER 1	READER 4	READER 7
READER 2	READER 5	
READER 3	READER 6	

....

READER 1: It takes a lot of letters to make up the alphabet,

READER 5: And two or three of them are very easy to forget;

READER 3: There's K, a funny letter, and X and Y and Z.

READER 7: There's hardly any use at all for any of those three!

READER 2: The vowels are the busy ones, A, E, I, O, U.

READER 6: They've twice the work that all the other letters have to do;

READER 4: I don't know why it is that grown-up people always choose

UNISON: To tell us children to be sure and mind our P's and Q's.

READER 7: They're funny looking letters, particularly Q,

READER 2: It never goes around except in company with U;

READER 5: P is much more important, it starts off pie and play,

READER 3: It's not hard to remember if you think of it that way;

READER 6: But lots of words begin with F and H and S and T,

READER 1: They're just as worth remembering as any, seems to me;

READER 4: Yet when we've strangers in the house, my parents always say,

UNISON: "Be sure you don't forget to mind your P's and Q's today!"

The Boy and the Wolf

John Hookham Frere

CHARACTERS

NARRATOR 1 NARRATOR 4
NARRATOR 2 BOY
NARRATOR 3 NEIGHBORS

NARRATOR 1: A little boy was set to keep
A little flock of goats or sheep.

NARRATOR 3: He thought the task too solitary,
And took a strange perverse vagary,

NARRATOR 2: To call the people out of fun,
To see them leave their work and run,

NARRATOR 4: He cried and screamed with all his might,

BOY: "Wolf! wolf!"

NARRATOR 4: in a pretended fright.

NARRATOR 2: Some people, working at a distance,
Came running in to his assistance.

NARRATOR 1: They searched the fields and bushes round,
The Wolf was nowhere to be found.

NARRATOR 3: The Boy, delighted with his game,
A few days after did the same,
And once again the people came.

NARRATOR 4: The trick was many times repeated,
At last they found that they were cheated.

NARRATOR 3: One day the wolf appeared in sight,
The Boy was in a real fright,

NARRATOR 1:   He cried,

BOY: "Wolf! wolf!"

NARRATOR 1:   The neighbors heard,
But not a single creature stirred.

NEIGHBORS: "We need not go from our employ,
(2 or more)   'Tis nothing but that idle boy."

NARRATOR 4:   The little boy cried out again,

BOY: "Help, help! the Wolf!"

NARRATOR 4:   he cried in vain.

NARRATOR 2:   At last his master went to beat him,
He came too late, the Wolf had eat him.

NARRATOR 4:   This shows the bad effects of lying,
And likewise of continual crying;

NARRATOR 1:   If I had heard you scream and roar,
For nothing, twenty times before,

NARRATOR 3:   Although you might have broke your arm,
Or met with any serious harm,
Your cries could give me no alarm,

NARRATOR 2:   They would not make me move the faster,
Nor apprehend the least disaster;

NARRATOR 1:   I should be sorry when I came,
But you yourself would be to blame.

The Lion and the Mouse
Jeffreys Taylor

.... **CHARACTERS** ....

        NARRATOR 1   NARRATOR 4
        NARRATOR 2   LION
        NARRATOR 3   MOUSE

....

NARRATOR 1: A Lion with the heat oppressed,
                One day composed himself to rest:

NARRATOR 4: But while he dozed as he intended,
                A mouse, his royal back ascended;

NARRATOR 2: Nor thought of harm, as AEsop tells,
                Mistaking him for someone else;

NARRATOR 3: And travelled over him, and round him,
                And might have left him as she found him

NARRATOR 4: Had she not, tremble when you hear,
                Tried to explore the monarch's ear!

NARRATOR 2: Who straightway woke, with wrath immense,
                And shook his head to cast her thence.

LION: "You rascal, what are you about?"

NARRATOR 1: Said he, when he had turned her out,

LION: "I'll teach you soon,"

NARRATOR 1: the lion said,

LION: "To make a mouse hole in my head!"

NARRATOR 3: So saying, he prepared his foot
                To crush the trembling tiny brute;

NARRATOR 2:   But she (the mouse) with tearful eye,
              Implored the lion's clemency,

MOUSE: "I ask, great sir, that you not eat me.
              Release me and some day I'll help thee."

NARRATOR 4:   The lion thought it best to give
              His little prisoner a reprieve.

NARRATOR 3:   'Twas nearly twelve months after this,
              The lion chanced his way to miss;

NARRATOR 1:   When pressing forward, heedless yet,
              He got entangled in a net.

NARRATOR 3:   With dreadful rage, he stamped and tore,
              And straight commenced a lordly roar;

NARRATOR 2:   When the poor mouse, who heard the noise,
              Attended, for she knew his voice.

NARRATOR 4:   Then what the lion's utmost strength
              Could not effect, she did at length;

NARRATOR 1:   With patient labor she applied
              Her teeth, the network to divide;

NARRATOR 2:   And so at last forth issued he,
              A lion, by a mouse set free.

NARRATOR 4:   Few are so small or weak, I guess,
              But may assist us in distress,

NARRATOR 3:   Nor shall we ever, if we're wise,
              The meanest, or the least despise.

The Grass

Emily Dickinson

CHARACTERS

READER 1
READER 2
READER 3
READER 4
READER 5

READER 1: The grass so little has to do,
A sphere of simple green,

READER 3: With only butterflies to brood,
And bees to entertain,

READER 5: And stir all day to pretty tunes
The breezes fetch along,

READER 4: And hold the sunshine in its lap
And bow to everything;

READER 2: And thread the dews all night, like pearls,
And make itself so fine,

READER 3: A duchess were too common
For such a noticing.

READER 5: And even when it dies, to pass
In odors so divine,

READER 1: As lowly spices gone to sleep,
Or amulets of pine.

READER 4: And then to dwell in sovereign barns,
And dream the days away,

READER 2: The grass so little has to do,

UNISON: I wish I were the hay!

© 2014 Susan Brown

The Jovial Welshmen

Author unknown

·· **CHARACTERS** ··

          NARRATOR 1   WELSHMAN 1

          NARRATOR 2   WELSHMAN 2

          NARRATOR 3   WELSHMAN 3

···

NARRATOR 1: There were three jovial Welshmen,
                     As I have heard them say,
               And they would go a-hunting
                     Upon St. David's Day.

NARRATOR 2: All the day they hunted,
                     But nothing could they find;
               But a ship a-sailing,
                     A-sailing with the wind.

NARRATOR 1: One said

WELSHMAN 1: it was a ship,

NARRATOR 3: The other he said

WELSHMAN 2: nay;

NARRATOR 2: The third said

WELSHMAN 3: it was a house,
                     With the chimney blown away.

NARRATOR 3: And all the night they hunted,
                     And nothing could they find
               But the moon a-gliding,
                     A-gliding with the wind.

NARRATOR 2: One said

WELSHMAN 1: it was the moon,

NARRATOR 1:   The other he said

WELSHMAN 2:   nay;

NARRATOR 3:   The other said

WELSHMAN 3:   it was a cheese,
    And half o't cut away.

NARRATOR 1:   And all the day they hunted,
    And nothing could they find,
But a hedgehog in a bramble bush,
    And that they left behind.

NARRATOR 3:   The first said

WELSHMAN 1:   it was a hedgehog,

NARRATOR 2:   The second he said

WELSHMAN 2:   nay;

NARRATOR 1:   The third

WELSHMAN 3:   it was a pin-cushion
    And the pins stuck in wrong way.

NARRATOR 2:   And all the night they hunted,
    And nothing could they find
But a hare in a turnip field,
    And that they left behind.

NARRATOR 3:   The first said

WELSHMAN 1:   it was a hare,

NARRATOR 2:   The second he said

WELSHMAN 2:   nay;

NARRATOR 1:   The third said

WELSHMAN 3:   it was a calf,
                     And the cow had run away.

NARRATOR 3:   And all the day they hunted,
                     And nothing could they find
                     But an owl in a holly tree
                     And that they left behind.

NARRATOR 1:   One said

WELSHMAN 1:   it was an owl,

NARRATOR 2:   The other he said

WELSHMAN 2:   nay;

NARRATOR 3:   The third said

WELSHMAN 3:   'twas an old man,
                     And his beard growing grey.

The Sorcerer's Apprentice
Johann Wolfgang von Goethe

························· **CHARACTERS** ·························

READER 1	READER 4	READER 7
READER 2	READER 5	READER 8
READER 3	READER 6	

··

READER 1: I am now, what joy to hear it,
              Of the old magician rid;

READER 3: And henceforth shall every spirit
              Do whatever by me is bid:

READER 5: I have watched with rigor
              All he used to do,

READER 7: And will now with vigor
              Work my wonders, too.

READERS 3 & 4: Wander, wander
                 Onward lightly,

READERS 7 & 8: So that rightly
                 Flow the torrent,

READERS 1 & 2: And with teeming waters yonder

READERS 5 & 6: In the bath discharge its current!

READER 2: And now come, you well-worn broom,
              And your wretched form bestir;

READER 4: You have ever served as groom,
              So fulfill my wishes, sir!

READER 7: On two legs now stand
              With a head on top;

READER 6: Water pail in hand,
      Haste and do not stop!

READERS 1 & 2: Wander, wander
      Onward lightly,

READERS 7 & 8: So that rightly
      Flow the torrent,

READERS 3 & 4: And with teeming waters yonder

READERS 5 & 6: In the bath discharge its current!

READER 8: See! he's running to the shore,
      And has now reached the pool,

READER 1: And with lightning speed once more
      Comes here, with his bucket full!

READER 4: Back he then repairs;
      See how swells the tide!

READER 5: How each pail he bears
      Straightway is supplied!

READERS 7 & 8: Stop, for lo!
      All the measure

READERS 3 & 4: Of your treasure
      Now is right!

READERS 5 & 6: Oh, I see it! woe, oh, woe!

READERS 1 & 2: I forgot the word of might.

READER 6: Oh, the word whose sound can straight
      Make him what he was before!

READER 2: Oh, he runs with nimble gait!
      Wish you were a broom once more!

READER 3:	Streams renewed forever Quickly they bring he;
READER 8:	River after river Rushes on poor me!
READERS 5 & 6:	Now no longer Can I bear him,
READERS 1 & 2:	I will snare him, Knavish sprite!
READERS 7 & 8:	Oh, my terror waxes stronger!
READERS 3 & 4:	What a look! what fearful sight!
READER 7:	Oh, you villain, where you dwell Shall the house through you be drowned
READER 4:	Floods I see that widely swell, Over the threshold gaining ground.
READER 1:	Will you not obey, Oh, you broom accursed!
READER 6:	Please be still, I say As you were at first!
READERS 7 & 8:	Will enough Never please you
READERS 3 & 4:	I will seize you, Hold you fast,
READERS 5 & 6:	And your nimble wood so tough
READERS 1 & 2:	With my sharp axe split at last.
READER 3:	See, once more he hastens back! Now, oh kobold, you shall catch it!

READER 5: I will rush upon his track;
    Crashing on him falls my hatchet.

READER 8: Bravely done, indeed!
    See, he's cleft in twain!

READER 6: Now from care I'm freed,
    And can breathe again.

READERS 1 & 2: Woe oh, woe!
    Both the parts,

READERS 5 & 6: Quick as darts,
    Stand on end,

READERS 3 & 4: Servants of my dreaded foe!

READERS 7 & 8: Someone please, protection send!

READER 5: And they run! and wetter still
    Grow the steps and grows the hall.

READER 8: Lord and master, hear me call!
    Ever seems the flood to fill.

READER 2: Ah, he's coming! see,
    Great is my dismay!

READER 7: Spirits raised by me
    Vainly would I lay!

READERS 3 & 4: "To the side
    Of the room

READERS 7 & 8: Hasten, broom,
    As of old!

READERS 1 & 2: Spirits I have never untied

READERS 5 & 6: Start to act as they are told."

www.ingramcontent.com/pod-product-compliance
Lightning Source LLC
LaVergne TN
LVHW081359060426
835510LV00016B/1907